Table of Contents

Chapter 1: About Crochet..
    History of Crochet..
    Language of Crochet..
    Basic Stitches 6
    Crochet Hooks 7
        Handling Crochet Hooks 8
        Hooks for Special Needs 8
        Hook Sizes..8
    Crochet Yarns 10
        Types of Yarns..11
Chapter 2: Tools and Materials 12
    Hooks 12
    Afghan Hook 12
    More About Yarns! 13
        Specialty Yarns..13
    Markers..14
    Tapestry Needles 14
        Joining Work 14
    Pins 15
    Tape Measure 16
    Row Counter 16
    Plastic Rings 16
    Metal Hook Gauge 17
    Bobbins 17
Chapter 3: Basic Techniques..18
    Practice, Practice, Practice! 18
    Catching the Yarn Technique 18
    Chain Stitch Technique (ch) 19
        Creating a Chain Stitch..20
    Single Crochet (sc) 20
    Half Double Technique (hdc) 21
    Double Crochet Technique (dc) 21
    Triple Crochet 22

Treble Crochet Technique (tr):	22
Turning Chains	23
The Button Stitch	23
Button Loops	24
Buttonhole Spacing	24
Sewing on Buttons	25
Cluster Stitch	25
Instructions:	25
Explanation:	25
Persian Stitch	26
Chapter 4: Some Great Crocheting Tips!	27
Bobbins	27
How to Make a Homemade Bobbin	27
Bouclé	27
Fastening Off	28
Randomly Crochet	28
Crocheters: Busy as Ever!	29
Some Crochet Innovations	30
Hairpin Lace	30
Tunisian Crochet	30
Broomstick Crochet	30
Crochet with Beads	30
Spool crochet	31
Random Crochet	31
Spread the Word; Share Your Love	31
Resources A-Bounty!	32
Conclusion	34

Chapter 1: About Crochet

History of Crochet

No one really knows when or how crochet actually came into being. This is because crochet, unlike knitting, was more a needle craft of the people - as opposed to the intricate lace knitting that was fashioned for royalty and the upper-class – then later preserved for museums and historians to study.

Throughout the centuries, crochet has stayed true to its roots and has always been a more accessible needle craft than knitting, as well as more versatile when it comes to the freedom of being able to create more imaginative and artistic garments, accessories, afghans, and other projects.

Historians agree that it was the lower classes who invented crochet. It's hard to believe now, but in the early history of the world, knitting needles and fine yarns and threads were only accessible to the very wealthy. That left anyone who was poor and wanted a hobby out of luck. Even when these materials became available to an emerging European middle class, it was only for the purpose of knitting to darn socks.

So an unrecorded and underground crochet movement simply began with people who found whatever kind of strands or threads they could and then used their fingers to make decorative knots and chains. This initial effort may have been closer to macramé than crochet, but it still became an affordable and creative craft for the masses.

Probably around the 1300's, people in Turkey, Persia, North Africa, China, and India began fashioning hooks out of either brass, bone, ivory, or wood. However, before people actually began "crocheting in the air" as it was called in France later on in the 1800's, another way of knotting and looping threads developed first.

Since no one knew that the crochet stitch could make a garment on its own, they turned to a method called "tambouring." This method was first developed in China and involves crochet-like stitches worked into fabric. It was around 1700 when garment makers would stretch a background fabric taught to a frame and then use a needle with a hook to push a loop of thread through the fabric. As the next loop was created, the hook was used join the loops together, thus creating the first chain stitch.

By the mid to late 1700's, enough of the original tambourine pieces had reached Europe from the orient to prompt Europeans to began to learn the craft of tambouring for themselves. Eventually, the fabric was eliminated and the upper class Europeans who had mastered the art of tambouring began using hooks made of silver, brass or steel to start creating the first modern crochet. Of course, once again, because it was only the upper class only who were allowed to crochet, the masses were left to continue to darn socks and dream of more creative outlets.

However, it was only a matter of time before the people learned to fashion their own hooks and get a hold of the odds and ends of thread needed to create ornamentation for their own garments. (When first evolving in Europe, it wasn't so much that crochet was being used to create whole garments as it was being used to decorate existing garments.)

The upper class, which made crochet fashionable, saw the emerging middle class and their new crochet and immediately declared it out of fashion. They promptly returned to the knitting that the lower classes could not afford and didn't return to crochet until Queen Victoria took up crochet herself and made it fashionable again.

While a more modern version of crochet originated from Italy and Spain, it was in the late 1700's that the French standardized crochet themselves and named it from the Middle French word 'croc' or 'croche' meaning 'hook.' The French also came out with the first patterns for garments by the year 1842. It was around this time that crocheted lace was also developed.

Later, standardized patterns that were easy to follow were then distributed. Although it would take some time to develop standardized needles, by the mid 1800's crochet had taken a firm hold as the most accessible way for the emerging middle class to pass the time in front of the fire while at the same time creating unique garments, accessories and home decorations.

Modern crochet still remains the needle-based craft of the people to this day. It is easy to learn, fun to do, and is much less restrictive than its stuffier knitting relative. In fact, one of the pursuits of more experienced crocheters is something called 'random crocheting.'

Random crocheting is the art of taking a pattern and altering it to make your own original creation. You can even start crocheting with an idea and simply see what happens. That's the beauty of crochet and what still makes it such a wonderful, satisfying and relaxing pursuit in this very modern and fast-paced world.

Language of Crochet

The language of crochet refers to the symbols and abbreviations used to create a pattern. There is nothing as exciting as finding a pattern that you love and the perfect yarn, and then sitting down to start your first project when you find some spare time. You may have even taken a seminar at the yarn store to get started.

Everything is so wonderful up to this point, that is, until you try to the read the pattern. This is because that unlike sewing, a crochet pattern is not visual. There are no drawings or easy pieces to cut out. A crochet pattern is simply a string of words and sentences that look something like an algebra story problem you avoided in high school.

It gets worse, because the sentences are incomplete and half of the words are abbreviations. Then, just for fun, the pattern maker throws in symbols which don't make any sense to novice crocheters. But take heart, it won't take you long to figure out the pattern once you know what everything means.

Just know that you are not alone when it comes to deciphering patterns and what they really mean for you to do. Some people get frustrated or give up at this point, but there is no need to panic. All you have to do is put away your yarn and needle for the moment and do a little bit of homework.

One of the best things to do is read through the entire pattern and make a note of everything you don't understand. Hopefully, you have picked out a very easy pattern for your first project like a scarf, a hat, or even a pot holder. Anything more complicated will just be frustrating.

Once you've read through the pattern and made notes of what you don't understand, you can use the following chart to decipher the abbreviations and symbols. Then, the next thing to do is write the pattern out in longhand. Doing this makes sure you understand the pattern and the whole project.

As well, if you write it out yourself, you can write it larger so you can see it easier and you won't have to be looking up directions for symbols or abbreviations. That way, you can concentrate on developing your crochet skills as opposed to getting frustrated by constantly flipping through a book looking for abbreviations.

Here is an example of how you can write out a pattern so you understand it:

Pattern:	Your Translation:
(dc, ch1, dc) in next sc	Place a double crochet, one chain stitch, and one more double crochet all in the next single crochet stitch from the previous row.

If you are really having problems with patterns, a great way to start is without one. Just crochet single and double stitches until you get the hang of it and then get the simplest pattern there is - a scarf. A scarf is just one piece of fabric crocheted in straight rows in whatever stitches you like. The best part is that you can make it as long or as short as you want and when it's finished you can say that you completed your first project.

With a scarf, you don't have to count rows, and it fits anyone so you can actually use it. You can learn to change colors and stitches and when you are finished you can put tassels on the ends just for fun. It's a project that you can give away as a gift or wear it yourself; and if anyone asks where you got it, you can proudly say, "I made this."

Basic Stitches

Abbreviation	Description	Abbreviation	Description
[ ]	work instructions within the brackets as many times as directed	g	gram
( )	work instructions within the brackets as many times as directed	hdc	half double crochet
*	repeat the instructions following the Single asterisk as directed	inc	increase/increases increasing
**	repeat instructions between asterisks as many times as directed	lp(s)	loops
"	inches	m	meter(s)
alt	alternate	MC	main color
approx	approximately	mm	millimeter(s)
beg	begin/beginning	oz	ounce(s)
bet	between	p	picot
BL	back loop(s)	pat(s) or patt	pattern(s)
bo	bobble	pc	popcorn
BP	back post	pm	place marker
BPdc	back post double crochet	prev	previous
Bpsc	back post single crochet	rem	remain/remaining
BPtr	back post treble crochet	rep	repeat(s)
Ca	color A	rnd(s)	round(s)
CB	color B	RS	right side
CC	contrasting color	sc	single crochet
ch	chain stitch	sc2tog	single crochet two stitches together
CL	cluster	sk	skip
cm	centimeter(s)	SL st	slip stitch
cont	continue	sp(s)	space(s)
dc	double crochet	st(s)	stitch(es)
dc2tog	double crochet 2 stitches together	tch or t-ch	turning chain
dec	decrease/decreases/decreasing	tbl	through back loop
dtr	double treble	tog	together
FL	front loop(s)	tr	treble crochet
foll	follow/follows/following	trtr	triple treble crochet
FP	front post	WS	wrong side
FPdc	front post double crochet	yd(s)	yard(s)
FPsc	front post single crochet	yo	yarn over
FPtr	front post treble crochet	yoh	yarn over hook

Crochet Hooks

Let's get started on your first project by understanding crochet hooks a little bit better. Obviously, crochet hooks are the needles with a hook on one end that that are used to pull the thread or yarn through the knotted loops of crochet for the purpose of creating stitches. Nevertheless, modern day crochet hooks have come a long way since they were made of bone and brass.

The most significant distinction between modern day crochet hooks and their historic predecessors is that hooks are now sized. This is extremely helpful, because with sized crochet hooks, there is no need to worry about sizing. Whether you are making a sweater or a table cloth, it will come out as the same size as the pattern if you use the recommended size crochet hook.

This is true for two reasons. First, the pattern will tell you the size of needle to use. Then it will tell you what kind of yarn to use if you want to create exactly what you see in the picture of the finished project that comes with the pattern.

Using the right size crochet hook will make sure that the stitches you make will be the same size as the pattern maker's stitches and essentially create a finished product that is the same size as the original. This is why it is important to use the same size crochet hook that the pattern maker uses if you want the exact same thing as you see in the picture that comes with the pattern.

Crocheting is a bit like cooking in the fact that if you are a beginner, you need to follow the directions exactly. For example, if you don't know how to cook, then you need to follow a recipe exactly in order to end up with a dish that is enjoyable to eat. An experienced cook can substitute and experiment here and there because they know what they are doing and may even come up with something better than the original; but an inexperienced cook who doesn't follow the directions exactly usually winds up ordering takeout.

So don't let your first crochet project become a disaster. Follow the directions exactly and you will be much more at peace with your finished creation. This also means buying the recommended yarn. You have to buy the right weight and the right amount of yarn (plus a little extra just in case) in order for the project to work. You may follow the directions exactly, but if you buy the wrong type or weight of yarn and use a different size crochet hook, you will wind up discouraged when the project doesn't turn out like you had hoped.

The size of the crochet hook and the weight of the yarn have been chosen by the pattern maker so that you will have the easiest time completing your project. This is why you need to stay away from specialty hooks and yarns that are difficult to work with. If you want to be creative, pick a fun color of yarn, but don't pick something like mohair or other yarns that are tricky to work with.

The best first pattern to use is one that calls for a medium size crochet hook and regular weight acrylic yarn. Once you have mastered your first project, you will be able to move onto more complicated projects that use all kinds of crochet hooks and specialty yarns.

Handling Crochet Hooks

Handling hooks at first is going to be very difficult. So don't be worry if your technique looks nothing like what it does in the crochet videos that you watch on the Internet. The first goal that you have is to get the stitches to look like they do in the diagrams that you see, so don't be afraid to hold the hook and yarn so that it is comfortable for you. Also, don't stress about using your fingers instead of the hook when you need to.

For example, it will be easier to make a slip knot with your fingers and put it on the hook when you are starting your foundation chain than it will be to hold the hook in one hand and the yarn in the other like it will show you in a video. That sort of dexterity comes with practice. As well, if your yarn splits or the stitch is too tight for the hook to pull through, take the hook out and pull it through with your fingers.

Hooks for Special Needs

If you have arthritis, carpal tunnel syndrome or other maladies that affect your grip, this doesn't preclude you from learning crochet. There are many specialty crochet hooks that you can buy that are ergonomically designed to ease the strain on the hands when you crochet. They are a little bit more expensive, but well worth the price if you want crochet.

Hook Sizes

If you ever wondered how a pattern for a sweater can always produce the same size sweater, it's because the needles used for the pattern come in standard sizes. When crochet was first popularized, there were standard patterns, but no standardized hooks.

This meant that someone really had to know what they were doing in order to produce a garment that would fit someone. Now hooks come in standardized sizes that let you produce the same garment or project so that it turns out exactly as the pattern. This is true as long as you use the same sized hook. There are also different hook sizes for different types of projects. In other words, you won't be using the same size hook to crochet lace as you will to crochet a heavy afghan.

Small hooks are used with thread to create lace patterns and are generally made of steel. You will most often use them to create doilies, table cloths, lace afghans, or even something like an heirloom wedding dress.

Larger hooks for afghans are made of aluminum, and even larger hooks for specialty yarns can be made of bamboo or plastic. These are for projects like accessories, sweaters, garments, and traditional afghans. The materials they are made of make them more light weight, durable and easier to handle. Here is a chart which has the measurements and sizes for both types of hooks - lace making hooks (steel) and regular sized hooks (aluminum, plastic or bamboo).

Steel Hooks

Millimeter Range	US Size Range*
.75 mm	14
.85 mm	13
1.0 mm	12
1.1 mm	11
1.3 mm	10
1.4 mm	9
1.5	8
1.65	7
1.8	6
1.9	5
2.0	4
2.1	3
2.25	2
2.75	1
3.25	0
3.5	00

Aluminum Hooks

Millimeter Range	US Size Range*
2.25mm	B-1
2.75 mm	C-2
3.25 mm	D-3
3.5 mm	E-4
3.75 mm	F-5
4 mm	G-6
4.5 mm	7
5 mm	H-8
5.5 mm	I-9
6 mm	J-10
6.5 mm	K-10 1/2
8 mm	L-11
9 mm	MN-13
10 mm	N/P-15
15 mm	P/Q
16 mm	Q
19mm	S

*Letter or number may vary. Rely on the millimeter (mm) sizing.

As you can see, there is a huge range of hook sizes, going from a tiny .75mm to a substantial 19mm. One of the great aspects of crochet is that is a very versatile craft. With the variety of needle sizes as well as the yarns and other materials you can use to crochet, the possibilities are endless.

Crochet Yarns

Shopping for yarn is a lot of fun because this is where you can imagine all of the wonderful things that you can make. You can probably spend hours at the yarn store, dreaming of all of the projects that you would like to start. A good yarn store will have all of the colors, weights and textures that you can imagine. As well, they will also have all of the idea books that will get your creative juices flowing.

It is so easy to get caught up in the moment that you may forget you are a beginner and wind up bringing home a project you can't complete. Remember, for your first projects it's okay to go to a superstore that happens to have a yarn section and pick up some regular weight yarn to practice with and use for your first projects.

This is because many people who go to the yarn store and pick out a harder project never wind up finishing it and may get turned off altogether. So if you have a good yarn store in your community, the first thing that you should do is not buy yarn, but sign up for classes. Crocheting is a great hobby to share with other people. That's how it got started in the first place.

Here are some yarn hints for beginning projects:

• Yarn Color: Forget about what your favorite colors are initially. Choosing a light color will help you see the stitches and get you crocheting faster.

• Yarn vs. Crochet Thread: If your only interest in crochet is making lace, then by all means start working with thread. However, if you are interested in crochet as a general pastime, it is easier to start working with regular weight yarn than it is to work with thread. As well, the patterns for lace can get complicated while regular weight yarn patterns are easier to read, execute and finish.

• Yarn Weights: The best yarns to start with are the acrylic worsted weights. They are easy to handle and less expensive if you don't plan on keeping your practice projects to use for anything. As well, if you wanted to start on a project like a throw rug or simple afghan, using higher weight yarns and larger size hooks is also a good idea.

International Yarn Weight Conversion

USA	UK	Australia	Suggested Needle
Laceweight	1 ply	2 ply	1.5-2.25 mm
Fingering	2 ply	3 ply	2.25-3 mm
Sock	3 ply	4 ply	2.25-3.25 mm
Sport	4 ply	5 ply	3.25-3.75 mm
DK/Light Worsted	DK	8 ply	3.75 – 4.5 mm
Worsted	Aran	10 ply	4.5 – 5.5 mm
Bulky	Chunky	12 ply	5.5 – 8 mm
Super Bulky	Super Chunky	14 ply	8 mm and up

This chart may not mean anything to you now, but you can use it for reference once you become a more advanced crocheter or start making your own patterns. For now, just beware that it exists in case you ever need it.

It is safe to say that all standardized patterns come with specific instructions for hook sizes, yarn weights and gauges; while all yarns and crochet hooks are clearly labeled with the corresponding hook sizes, yarn weights and gauges as well. So shopping for yarn supplies and patterns, even if you go to a department store, is easy to do without any help.

Types of Yarns
Yarn can be spun out of almost any fiber, which makes the possibilities for projects almost endless. However, the three most common types of yarn that you will probably be dealing with are acrylic, cotton and wool.

- Acrylic Yarn: Acrylic yarn usually gets a bad rap because when you say acrylic yarn people think of the kitschy afghans and sweaters from the 1970's. However, while you should always steer clear of cheap acrylics, there are so many advances in colors, weights, and textures that you shouldn't automatically tune acrylics out just because of the stigma attached to them. The reason to stay away from cheap acrylics is that they can be as hard to work with as some of the specialty fibers. They can knot, catch and split apart easily. However, the high end acrylics have many advantages. They don't fade or shrink, don't usually produce allergic reactions, wear well for a longer period of time, and can go through the washer and dryer.

- Wool Yarn: Wool is one of the most popular yarns for both crocheters and knitters alike. This is because not only is wool resilient, it shows fewer mistakes. Your projects will last longer and wear better; and if you want to hand them down to future generations, there is a certain cachet to having heirloom crafts made of wool. Wool is also easier to work with, so it is recommended that unless you are allergic, do all your practice work with a skein of wool. The thing about wool is that you can practice something like single crochet, rip out all of the stitches, and use the same yarn over and over.

- Cotton Yarn: Cotton is a popular natural fiber as well, but you have to be careful about the projects you select when you choose to work with cotton. This is because crochet, unlike knitting, can create an inelastic fabric. As well, cotton yarn is an inelastic fiber. So when you combine the two, you come up with an absolutely inelastic fabric. This makes white cotton perfect for projects like tablecloths and accessories like purses, but not so great for sweaters. Note: If you are allergic to wool, cotton is the next best natural fiber to practice with when you are first starting out.

Chapter 2: Tools and Materials

One of the reasons that crochet was originally popular with the masses was that it was so inexpensive. While there are supplies that you will need to purchase, depending on where you shop, you can get started on your own for less than ten dollars.

If you know someone who crochets or find a crochet group, they will start you off with supplies for free. Crocheters are just that kind of people and welcome anyone new to their group with open arms. As well, patterns on the Internet are free; so while the following chapter is a description of supplies that you will need as you eventually get more experienced, by all means feel free to go to the store, get a hook and some cheap acrylic yarn and start crocheting!

Hooks

Probably, when you first start out practicing crochet, you will only buy one hook and one skein of yarn unless you have a specific project in mind. If you do only buy one hook for practice, the best hooks to buy are either a size "G" or "H", but understand that it is only the beginning.

Many novice crocheters make the mistake of holding onto their original hook and only using it instead of expanding. As you become more experienced, not only does using one hook limit the amount of projects you can make, but it also may get you into bad habits when you crochet; like making stitches that are too tight and too loose to be able to produce an accurate gauge. This will be a problem when you do move onto more advance projects and other sizes of needles.

The advice here is that as soon as you feel comfortable enough to move on from practicing to projects, you should buy a range of needles and learn how to use them. This means from the delicate lace needles all the way up to the larger bulky needles. The reason for this is to keep you versatile and always enjoying new challenges when you crochet. The great thing, once again, about crochet is that a set of crochet hooks is very inexpensive. There are individual hooks which can be a bit pricey, but a standard set is relatively cheap.

Afghan Hook

An afghan hook is used for afghan-stitch crochet, which is also known as Tunisian crochet. This is crochet that originated in the Mediterranean so not only is it one of the older and more original versions of crochet, it is unique in the fact that it didn't evolve like modern day crochet so the stitches and the look of the fabric have a distinct flair. Remember, before France popularized crochet, Spain, Italy and North Africa already had their own versions of crochet which they kept in intact.

The Afghan hook looks like a knitting needle with a hook on the end of it. When you use an afghan hook, as in knitting, you keep all of the stitches on the hook as you work them on the first pass of a row. Then on the second pass, you work them off of the needles. The knob at the end of the hook keeps all of the stitches on while they are on the hook.

The work is never turned as there is no need to and is always worked on the right side. Some people confuse the afghan hook with a cro-hook, but a cro-hook is just a crochet needle with a hook on either end and is used when working two colors at the same time.

More About Yarns!

There are so many different kinds of yarns to work with once you become an experienced crocheter that you will never run out of different kinds of projects to try. Between patterns, stitches and yarns there are infinite possibilities for new and exciting combinations to produce diverse results.

Specialty Yarns

These are the yarns that make beautiful and interesting projects, but they are not for beginners. With these yarns, it is hard to see the stitches, easy to knot them up and hard to take them apart if you make a mistake.

- Fleece: This yarn is spun from the shed or collected hair of animals and includes Angora (rabbits) and Kashmir (goats).

- Novelty: *Bouclé:* This is a very popular textured 3 ply yarn with bumps and loops.
Chenille: A soft, fuzzy yarn that can be made from synthetic or natural fibers.
Eyelash Yarn: This is base thread which has fluffy strands to create the look of fur when crocheted or knitted.
Railroad Ribbon: Two strands of thread are joined by what looks like tiny tracks.
Ribbon: Rayon strands which have been knitted into a ribbon.
Thick-Thin: Sections of yarn go from thick to thin and create an uneven fabric.

- Specialty: *Heather:* Different fleeces are blended and then dyed to match.
Marled: This yarn is made from plies of different colors.
Tweed: A solid color yarn with flecks of other colors.
Variegated: A yarn that has different colors alternated in the same skein.

In addition to using specialty yarns, a really creative crafter can crochet with just about anything. If you look back through history, the original crocheters started crocheting with any odds and ends they could find. Modern day crocheters can use raffia, corn husks, plastic bags, string, rags, fabric, terry cloth, paper or any other material that is pliable. Literally, the sky is the limit when it comes to material you can use to crochet!

Markers

Markers for crochet and knitting are used in specific instances. It is important to use markers whenever you are crocheting in the round such as when you are making something like doilies or coasters. You use a marker on every round because otherwise you wouldn't be able to find the beginning of it, and if you ever have to hand count stitches, especially if you are making lace or using specialty yarn, you will understand why.

Markers are also used when making hats, socks and any other projects where you need to mark pattern repeats. As well, markers help with specialty yarns like chenille, eyelash yarns and Bouclé.

Crochet markers can be purchased, but there isn't really a need to do this. A marker can simply be a piece of thread that is inserted into the stitch as you complete a round. Although, the advantage of store bought markers is that you can't accidently pull one out as easily as you can a piece of thread.

Tapestry Needles

Tapestry needles are blunt, heavy-duty needles that are used for joining work together. They can be purchased at any craft or department store and chances are you may already have one if you have a sewing kit. You will need to use a tapestry needle to join work in the case of any project that has multiple pieces like a sweater or a stuffed animal. There are several methods for using a tapestry needle to join pieces together. The way you will use it will depend on the type of yarn you are using and what the finished creation will be used for after it is completed.

Joining Work
The first thing to do when joining work, especially with clothing, is to pin the pieces that you are going to join together with the right sides facing and make sure they are matched up stitch to stitch. This is because you are going to use the tapestry needle to join each individual stitch together and if you want a professional looking seam, they have to match exactly. To get started, thread the tapestry needle with matching yarn, or contrasting yarn if you want to put the wrong sides facing each other and use the stitching as ornamentation.

- Whip Stitch Finishing: Insert the threaded tapestry needle into the loops of the stitches that are touching each other and work down the entire seam. For a sturdier but bulkier seam, pass the threaded needle through all four loops of every stitch.

- Back Stitch Seam: With a backstitch seam, the threaded needle is inserted under the stitches. Insert the needle under both sets of the first stitch (front to back) and pull the thread tight. Insert the needle into the next stitch (front to back) and continue until you reach the end of the seam.

● Woven Seam: With the least noticeable seam, the two pieces of fabric are laid next to each other and the tapestry needle is used to make an "S" shape with the yarn to join the pieces together. Insert the tapestry needle into the first stitches and pull the thread through. Then, making a 'u-turn,' go into the next stitches in the row, pulling the thread through again. Repeat until you reach the end of the seam, but don't pull too tight because this is meant to be a stretchy stitch.

Pins

Pins are used at some point in any sort of needle work, but in crochet they are for a specific purpose. Although you use pins to help assemble pieces on a project like sweaters, they are really more important to use before you join the pieces together. This is when you use the pins to block the fabric pieces.

Blocking is the process that is used before assembling the pieces of a sweater or other garment. It is the most important step of making a sweater, which turns it from a homemade looking eyesore into a professional looking garment.

Blocking is the process of wetting the individual pieces and laying them flat on a padded surface; then stretching and pinning them so that they are the exact measurements of the pattern. Then the pieces must be left to dry thoroughly (least 24 to 48 hours) before they are assembled. Letting the piece dry thoroughly is the key to successful blocking.

The pieces can be wetted in the sink and then pinned down to dry or you can pin them down dry and wet them with a spray bottle, steamer or steam iron. However, if you use a steam iron, make sure that you use a pressing cloth and use the following guidelines to make sure that you do not harm the crochet pieces.

Angora	Wet block by spraying
Cotton	Wet block or warm/hot steam press
Linen	Wet block or warm
Lurex	Do not block
Mohair	Wet block by spraying
Novelties	Do not block, unless instructed
Synthetics	Wet block by spraying
Wool and wool-like fibers	Wet block by spraying or press warm
Wool blends	Wet block by spraying; do not press

The best kinds of pins to buy are rust proof pins with glass heads. They are larger pins so they are easier to use and they won't rust onto the garment when they have been wet for a few days.

Tape Measure

The tape measure is used in crocheting for different reasons:

1. You can take your own measurements to know your garment size.
2. You need it for blocking.
3. You need it to measure your gauge sample.

A gauge sample is a practice piece that you make before you start every project to make sure that your finished piece will be the same size as the pattern. This is especially important if you are making garments. On every pattern that you work there will be what is called a gauge. The gauge is a measurement that tells you how many stitches there are per inch or millimeter. A sample gauge looks something like this: *18 sts to 4"pattern worked on size F hook.*

The translation is that you will use a size F hook which will create 4 inches of crochet fabric with every 18 stitches that you make. So if you go buy this example and the pattern calls for single crochet and worsted weight yarn, you would take your worsted weight yarn and crochet a sample of 18 stitches and about three or four rows. Use the tape measure to check the sample and make sure that it is 4 inches wide. If it isn't, then you need to make sure that the stitches aren't too tight or too loose.

If you can't get it right after a few attempts, you may need to change the needle size. Remember that while patterns, hooks and yarns are all standardized, everyone crochets differently. To get the gage right, try one needle size up or down, depending on whether your stitches are too tight or too loose. This is why it is a good idea that once you start doing projects to buy a whole set of needles instead of just a few sizes.

Row Counter

A row counter is a device that is used to count the rows when you are crocheting. It is especially helpful if you are new to crochet and don't exactly know what a row looks like. To use the row counter, you simply click the add row button every time you start a new row. A row counter is also helpful if you are working in the round or working with specialty yarns like eyelash yarns or chenille.

Plastic Rings

Sometime when you are working in the round or working on a specific craft project, you may need to crochet over a plastic ring. This is an awkward proposition at first, but once you get the hang of it, it becomes really easy.

To crochet around a plastic ring, first make a slipknot and place it around the hook. Holding the ring in the left hand, insert the hook into the ring front to back. With the hook pushed through the ring, yarn over and then pull the hook back through the ring. Your hook will be back on the right side with the slip knot and the yarn over loop on it. Next take the hook to the top of the ring and yarn over again. To complete the first single crochet, pull through both loops on the hook. Repeat until the ring is covered.

Metal Hook Gauge

Metal hooks aren't as durable as aluminum. They can bend and break, but if you use them repeatedly, the size can also wear off. As well, if a hook is older it may not have a size on it; but that doesn't mean you can't use it.

A metal hook guage is a handheld piece of cardboard or plastic that has holes in it that are marked with the different sizes for metal hooks. All you have to do is stick the unidentified hook into the holes until you find a match. That way, if you find an old hook at a garage sale or if an older relative or friend gives you unmarked metal hooks, you can still use them.

Bobbins

Crochet bobbins are used for working with a pattern that uses multiple colors of yarn. When you start working with multiple colors and you don't know about bobbins, you may try to have three or four skeins going as you switch colors and try to keep all of the skeins from getting tangled and knotted.

Crochet bobbins are small spools that hold a smaller amount of yarn so that your different yarns won't get tangled. While you can always cut the yarns at any time, it is usually easier to run the colors on the wrong side of the work and keep the bobbins hanging off the back so you don't have a lot of loose ends to finish off when you are finished.

Chapter 3: Basic Techniques

Practice, Practice, Practice!

There is no way around it. Crochet, like any other needle work, takes practice. First, you have to practice the chain stitch and then the single crochet stitch. However, once you know the double crochet stitch, you can make many different projects. That's the beauty of crochet.

In one afternoon, you should be able to do single crochet, even though it will be uneven and not look perfect. Still, you will feel a sense of accomplishment and know that bigger projects are within your grasp, though you will still need more practice.

A great way to practice is the scarf project that was mentioned earlier. Because like most people, if you find practice boring, at least you can practice your single and double crochet and have a purpose.

So take a day and go yarn shopping. You can buy fun colors and even pick up a few specialty yarns if you want. Then you can practice with a purpose. Making scarves for your family and friends is a great way to practice, give gifts and let people admire your handiwork all at the same time!

You can also try potholders, pillows and anything else that comes in a square. Also, if you really like practicing, you can make an afghan. It doesn't matter what it looks like. The important thing is that you made it.

Note: Afghans made of squares that you need to join together is a good way to practice blocking and joining seams.

Catching the Yarn Technique

As you are practicing, you will need to work on feeding the yarn. Feeding the yarn is very important, because it must be looped around the crochet hook the right way or your work may become too tight to work with or too loose to stay together.

Catching the yarn (in patterns it is called yarn over or y/o) is the way to feed the yarn into the existing fabric by creating new loops. To get started with a foundation chain, make a slip knot on your hook. Take the hook in your right hand and the yarn in your left, letting it drape loosely over your left hand.

With the yarn draped over your left index finger, move the yarn behind the hook and drape the yarn over it – back to front so that it catches on the hook. Still holding the yarn in your left hand, pull the yarn that is on the hook through the slip knot already on the hook in order to start a chain stitch. This will be very awkward at first, but one of the tedious things you need to practice in order to get better at crochet.

Chain Stitch Technique (ch)

The chain stitch is the basis for all crochet work and the best way to get started with crochet. Working on the chain stitch is also a great way to develop the way you handle your crochet hook.

There are two ways to hold a crochet hook and both ways are acceptable. In fact, many people who crochet will hold the hook one way for a while and then change up so that their hands don't get tired.

The first way to hold a crochet hook is called the "pencil grip" which, as the title implies, means that you hold the crochet hook as you would a pencil in your dominant hand. The other way to hold a crochet hook is called the "knife grip" which means that you hold the crochet hook in your dominate hand as you would a knife while cutting meat.

If you can't visualize this, there are many websites with diagrams where you can go that have pictures of the two different ways to hold a hook. You will find a list of these websites in the back of this publication.

As well, crochet hooks don't come as left handed or right handed so you can hold the hook in either hand. The only thing to remember is to substitute left for right, as most crochet directions are unfortunately written for right-handed people.

Note: A good size crochet hook to start with to practice is the size 'H' hook and a 4-ply acrylic yarn.

To start a chain hold the crochet hook in your dominate hand and the end of the yarn in the other. All crochet begins with a chain as the foundation, so it is very important that you take the time to learn to do it right, as every row afterwards depends on the quality of the chain.

Just the same, every piece of crochet begins with a slip knot, so this is where you begin to crochet. To make a slip knot, simply make a loop with the end of the yarn. Put the crochet hook through the loop and then pull the end through the loop. Hold the crochet hook in your right hand and both ends of the yarn in your left hand, and then pull gently on both sides until you have a loose slip knot on the hook of the needle. You are now ready to create a chain stitch.

Creating a Chain Stitch

Hold the crochet hook in your right hand with slip knot about ½" away from the hook using either the pencil or knife method. Wrap the long end of the yarn loosely around your left hand. Use your left forefinger and thumb to hold the loose end of the yarn to keep it taught. Then wrap the long end of the yarn around the back of the hook so that it rests right under the hook in such a way that you can pull it through the slip knot tied onto the hook.

This is called 'yarn over hook', abbreviated as 'y/o'. 'Yarn over hook' puts the yarn in a position whereby you can pull the yarn through the loop on the hook and create the next stitch. So at this point you can pull the yarn on the hook through the loop (or slipknot on the hook) and create your first chain stitch.

Remember to let the long end of the yarn go as you pull it through the loop. This will be extremely awkward the first time you do it, but don't get frustrated. It will probably be a good idea to spend an entire afternoon practicing your chain stitch and getting used to working with the yarn and hook. This is a good time to make sure your technique is correct, because once you get to harder patterns you will need to make sure you are using the proper form.

To make a chain, just keep wrapping the long end of the yarn around the hook and pulling it thought the loop while you hold the short end taught in your left hand. This is where practice comes in, because while both ends of the yarn are held in the left hand; the short end of the yarn must remain taught while the long end of the yarn must remain loose so the gauge is correct.

Single Crochet (sc)

After you have mastered the chain stitch, you are ready to start learning more basic stitches that will build on the chain foundation and allow you to crochet. In fact, once you have mastered the foundation chain stitch, single crochet, and finally the slip stitch; you will be able to crochet many different simple projects.

Single crochet is used in different ways. It can either be used to create a firm, flat fabric or it can be used to join different pieces together - like if you are making a sweater. It can also be used to finish off the edges of a piece, like the border on an afghan.

To learn single crochet, make a chain of thirty stitches. Don't make your chain any longer because it will be difficult to work with. Also make sure to keep the stitches loose. A tight chain will make it hard to insert and withdraw the hook from the chain stitches.

At the end of the chain, make one extra stitch for a total of 31. This last stitch is the turning stitch, which as the name implies, allows for turning. Now you will create your single crochet by working back along the foundation chain.

Begin your single crochet by inserting the hook front to back into the second chain stitch from the hook. In other words, you are skipping the turning stitch and inserting the hook into the last foundation chain stitch you created. There will now be two loops on your hook. This will be the turning stitch and the last chain stitch you created.

Wrap the yarn coming from the skein around the hook and with a smooth, single movement, and then pull the yarn on the hook back through both loops on the hook to create a single loop on the hook with the new supply of yarn. You have just created your first single crochet. Continue to the end of the chain to create your first row of single crochet.

When you reach the end of the row you will need to create another turning stitch which does not count if you are counting stitches. To create a turning stitch, simply make one chain stitch and continue your single crochet by working in the first single crochet stitch from the previous row. If you do not make a turning stitch, your work will be bunched up on the ends and not lie flat.

Half Double Technique (hdc)

Half double crochet is mainly used when creating garments. This is because while it is taller than single crochet, it is firmer than double crochet. It also has a more appealing texture for garments than either single or double crochet.

There are two steps to working the half double technique. The first is working along the foundation chain and the next is working along the half double rows themselves. To practice, make your foundation chain of 30 stitches, but this time you will make two turning stitches on the end for a total of thirty two.

Using the forefinger of your left hand, wrap over the long end of the yarn all the way around the hook in your right hand. Insert the hook (front to back) in the third loop from the hook. You now have three loops on the hook. Do another wrap around on the hook and pull it back through all three loops. You now created your first half double crochet stitch.

Work your half double technique all the way down the chain until you reach the end, and then crochet two chains to turn the work. Skip these two stitches and work in the first half double stitch from the previous row. You will work one half double stitch into every half double stitch on that row. Every time you get to the end of the row, remember to make two turning chain stitches and start work in the first turning chain stitch from the previous row.

Double Crochet Technique (dc)

To practice the double crochet technique, make your foundation chain of 30 stitches, and this time you will make two turning stitches on the end for a total of thirty two.

Using the forefinger of your left hand, wrap over the long end of the yarn all the way around the hook in your right hand. Insert the hook (front to back) in the third loop from the hook. You now have three loops on the hook. Do another wrap around on the hook and pull it back through the stitch. You will still have three loops on the hook.

Wrap the yarn around the hook and pull it through the first two stitches on the hook, leaving the last loop on the hook. There will now be two loops on the hook. Wrap the yarn around it around the hook one last time and pull it through the remaining two loops. You now created your first double crochet stitch.

Work your double technique all the way down the chain until you reach the end, and then crochet two chains to turn the work. Skip these two stitches and work in the first double stitch from the previous row. You will work one half double stitch into every half double stitch on that row. Every time you get to the end of the row, remember to make two turning chain stitches and start work in the first turning chain stitch from the previous row.

Triple Crochet

For triple crochet, simply wrap the yarn around the needle twice before inserting it into the stitch and then take off the stitches two at a time like the double. Because you have wrapped around the hook twice before inserting it into the stitch there will be three sets of double loops to take off, which will create the triple crochet. Keep in mind that when working triple crochet, you will need to make four turnaround chain stitches when you turn the work in order for it lay flat and not bunch up. As well, you will need four extra chain stitches and on the first triple crochet on the chain, and you will insert the hook into the fifth stitch from the chain.

Treble Crochet Technique (tr):

To practice the treble crochet technique, make your foundation chain of 30 stitches, but this time you will make 4 turning stitches on the end for a total of thirty four.

Using the forefinger of your left hand, wrap over the long end of the yarn all the way around the hook in your right hand twice to create two 'loops' on the hook. Insert the hook (front to back) in the fifth loop from the hook. You now have four loops on the hook. Do another wrap over on the hook and pull it back through the stitch. You will now have four loops on the hook. Do another wrap over and pull off two stitches from the hook. You will now have three stitches on the hook. Wrap over the hook again and pull off two more stitches. There will be two final loops on the hook. Wrap over the hook and pull of the last two. This completes your first treble stitch.

Work your treble crochet technique all the way down the chain until you reach the end, and then crochet four chains to turn the work. Skip these four stitches and work in the first treble stitch from the previous row. You will work one treble stitch into every treble stitch on that row. Every time you get to the end of the row, remember to make four turning chain stitches and start work in the first turning chain stitch from the previous row.

Turning Chains

Turning chain stitches are the chain stitches that you create in order to turn your work and begin the next row. The reason you make chain stitches when you turn your work is to bring your yarn to the height necessary to work the next row of stitches. Otherwise the ends of the work would be bunched up and the piece will not lie flat. The numbers of chain stitches you need to take at the end of which row depends on what stitch you are working. This is because each stitch is a different height. Following is a chart to refer to in case you have questions:

Stitch Name and Abbreviation	Number of Turning Chains Needed
Slip Stitch (sl st)	0
Single Crochet (sc)	1
Half Double Crochet (hdc)	2
Double Crochet	3
Triple Crochet	4
Double Triple Crochet	5

Except for single crochet, the turning chain from the previous row always counts as the first stitch of the next row. In the case of single crochet, always work the first single crochet stitch in the row instead of the chain stitch. This will fill out the rows on the end and keep them even.

The Button Stitch

There are several ways to make a buttonhole, depending on the type of garment you are making. If you are crocheting in a single crochet stitch, when you get to the place where the button hole is supposed to be - chain one stitch, skipping over the next single crochet stitch and picking up the stitch after. This creates a hole for the button to push through when you go to fasten up the garment. When you crochet the next row, treat the chain stitch as if it were a single crochet stitch as you are working the row.

After you complete the first single crochet on the row with the button hole, work about 4 more single crochet and then stop to test the button you will be using with the garment. The button hole should neither be too loose nor too tight. If the single stitch button hole you have created is too small, unravel the four or five stitches you have created and chain as many stitches as you need to fit the button through the hole comfortably.

If you need more than one chain stitch to fit a button, make sure to pick up the single crochet stitch that matches the number of chain stitches you have created. For example, if you make three chain stitches to create a button hole for a larger button, then skip three stitches and resume with single crochet where you left off.

Button Loops

Button loops for a delicate cardigan are another button solution. First, you will join the yarn that will create the button loops with a slip stitch to the top of the lapel edge of the cardigan where you want the button holes to start. The next step is to slip stitch or single crochet down to where the *bottom* of the first button loop should be. Turn the work and crochet a chain that will fit the button; then attach it to the top of the button hole.

For reinforcement, single crochet down the *button loop* to the bottom of the loop and reinforce it to the sweater with a slip stitch. Continue to single crochet down the lapel to the next place for a button loop and repeat until all of the button loops are in place. Continue to the bottom of the garment and finish off.

Buttonhole Spacing

There nothing like finishing your first sweater and finding that the buttonholes aren't spaced evenly. To prevent this, you will need to measure where the button holes go and place markers on your work to get them in the right place.

If the button holes are right on the front of the cardigan, then you will have to count rows. The buttons should be an equal number of rows apart so make sure to count the rows and keep track of how many rows are between each button. The pattern will tell you where to put the top and bottom button hole, but it won't tell you where to place the other button holes, so it is important to keep count. This is especially true if you have an situation where there is an odd number of buttons and an even number of rows or any other situation where the math doesn't quite work out.

If there is a button band that is crocheted into the cardigan, the button holes will be made vertically. This will require measuring with a tape measure and marking the button band with markers like pins to make sure the distance between the button holes is equal. Again, the crochet pattern will tell you where to put the top button hole and the bottom one, but you have to measure where the other button holes will be placed.

Sewing on Buttons

The pattern also won't explain how to sew on the buttons, just that it needs to be done. Buttons that are merely sewn onto a crocheted sweater will quickly pull it out of shape. The trick here is to buy the fashion buttons that will go on the front of the cardigan or jacket and then buy the same number of shirt buttons that will secure them to the back.

To attach a backup button, have the fashion button on the right side of the crocheted fabric and the shirt button behind it on the wrong side. Sew the two buttons together, going through the fabric and their corresponding holes. You now have a backup button that will take the stress off of the crocheted fabric of the cardigan. Note : the backup buttons should be a matching color.

Cluster Stitch

To practice the cluster stitch, make your foundation chain of 30 stitches, without any turning stitches. Because cluster stitches vary from pattern to pattern, the directions will tell you how many stitches to make to form your cluster stitch by using the ** symbols to tell you how many time to repeat the stitch. This example shows how to make a cluster with four double crochet. Following, please find the directions and then an explanation.

Instructions:

1. *Yarn over, insert hook in next stitch, yarn over, draw yarn through the stitch, yarn over, draw though 2 loops on hook*, repeat from * to * 3 times.
2. Yarn over; draw yarn through five loops on hook.

Explanation:

Using the forefinger of your left hand, wrap over the long end of the yarn all the way around the hook in your right hand. Insert the hook (front to back) in the first loop from the hook. You now have three loops on the hook. Do another yarn over on the hook and pull it back through the stitch. You will still have three loops on the hook.

Wrap the yarn around the hook and pull it through the first two stitches on the hook, leaving the last loop on the hook. There will now be two loops on the hook. Using the forefinger of your left hand, wrap over the long end of the yarn all the way around the hook in your right hand. Reinsert the hook (front to back) in the first loop from the hook. Make sure the loops are loose so you will be able to do this.

Do another wrap over on the hook and pull it back through the stitch. You will now have four loops on the hook. Wrap the yarn around the hook and pull it through the first two stitches on the hook, leaving the last loop on the hook. You will now have three loops on the hook.

Using the forefinger of your left hand, wrap over the long end of the yarn all the way around the hook in your right hand. Reinsert the hook (front to back) in the first loop from the hook. Do another wrap around on the hook and pull it back through the stitch. You will now have five loops on the hook. Do another rap over and pull the yarn through two loops. You now have four loops on your hook.

Using the forefinger of your left hand, wrap over the long end of the yarn all the way around the hook in your right hand. Reinsert the hook (front to back) in the first loop from the hook. Do another wrap over on the hook and pull it back through the stitch. Wrap the yarn around the hook and pull it through the first two stitches on the hook. You will now have five stitches on the hook. Do a final yarn over and pull it through all five stitches. Congratulations! You have created your first cluster.

Persian Stitch

The Persian stitch, like the cluster stitch, is a decorative stitch that is usually used in conjunction with a pattern like an afghan or a sweater where some decorative stitching will dress up an otherwise basic pattern. This is a more advanced stitch, so don't worry if you don't get it right the first couple of times.

With the Persian stitch, you will already be in the middle of the row, so it has nothing to do with turning chains or anything like that. Instead you will be working with something like single or double crochet - which is why the Persian stitch uses the left and right hand side of the stitch to make loops.

Insert the hook (front to back) in the first loop from the hook on the left hand side. Using the forefinger of your left hand, wrap over the long end of the yarn all the way around the hook in your right hand and pull it through the stitch. Repeat on the right hand side of the stitch. You will now have three loops on the hook. Yarn over and pull the thread through all three loops on the hook.

Draw another loop through the left thread of the new stitch and then and another loop through the next stitch in the row. Yarn over and pull the thread through all three loops. The pattern will give you your next instructions.

While this instruction may sound a little vague, the Persian stitch is really specific to the patterns that use it and more instruction will be given to when you really need to use the Persian stitch.

Chapter 4: Some Great Crocheting Tips!

There is so much more to crocheting than just following the written directions and patterns. There are shortcuts and substitutions and solutions that no one could possibly cover in one or even several books. This is why the Internet is such a great tool for the crochet community.

If you don't know anyone or don't have crocheting in your area, you can go online twenty four hours a day and talk to crochet experts who know what they are talking about. In the meantime, here are a few helpful tips to get you started.

Bobbins

How to Make a Homemade Bobbin

Yarn bobbins aren't really expensive, but it is always nice to save money when there are other options besides buying more crochet accessories. To make a bobbin to hang off the back of your work when you are changing colors, simply take a piece of cardboard and cut it in the shape of an H. Make a notch on one of the legs to anchor the yarn. To use it, hook the yarn in the notch and wrap the yarn around the middle and begin crocheting the yarn into your work. The cardboard is light enough to hang off the back of your work and an inexpensive and quick way to manage the different colored yarns on your crochet project.

Pattern for a Homemade Bobbin

Bouclé

The term Bouclé can refer to either the yarn or the fabric created by it. It comes from the French word *boucler* meaning 'to curl.' Bouclé is a specialty yarn that is made from three plies: two that are spun like worsted yarn and one that is loose. This loose ply is what gives Bouclé its nubby and uneven texture. What is beautiful about Bouclé is that when it is crocheted, it neither looks like knitting or crochet, but rather an exotic type of material. The finished project has a much more professional and interesting look, and the stitches are much less defined.

This is why many crocheters rush to use Bouclé for their first projects. However, the same thing that makes Bouclé one of the nicest yarns to use for a project also makes it the worst. Because of the third and loose strand, Bouclé is extremely difficult to work with. You can't see the stitches and it knots easily - so if you make a mistake, you may not be able to get it out.

Don't despair though, the test to know when you are ready to work with Bouclé will be when you can crochet with worsted and watch television at the same time without thinking about what you are doing. While it sounds like a funny kind of test, it's really true. When you are completely comfortable with regular worsted yarn, it's time to move on to the exciting world of Bouclé.

Fastening Off

Fastening off is a satisfying part of the project because it means that you are almost done. When you work the last stitch of the project it is time to finish off so you don't have any loose ends. To finish off, cut the end of the yarn six inches from the hook, and then draw it back through the last loop on the hook to create a slip knot.

Pull on the yarn gently to make a snug knot. Thread the end of the yarn that is left attached to the project onto a yarn needle and weave it into the tops of a few of the stitches. Weave back a few more stitches and cut the yarn about ¼ from the fabric and gently pull on the fabric to make the tail end of the yarn disappear. Finishing off not only gives the project a professional look, but it also makes it hard for it to unravel.

Randomly Crochet

Randomly crocheting has breathed new life into crochet and brought a new breed and generation of crocheters into the fold. Random crocheting means just what is says: it is crocheting without a pattern and going where the spirit takes you. Of course, this was how crochet originated; with people freely creating crocheted ornamentation to sew on their garments without any pattern and using odds and ends of materials they would find.

There are two different schools of thought on random crochet, the first being to take a pattern and make it your own. For example, if you want to make a pair of baby booties you might make the sole of the shoe from a pattern. This is practical, because you want the shoe to fit a certain size foot. At this point, however, the pattern is thrown out and the rest of the booty is made from the imagination.

Again, in the case of a garment, it has to be wearable, and in the case of a shoe or a glove you will have to write down what you did so that you can replicate it. Still, there is a great satisfaction in doing so and random crocheting is drawing in younger artistic types who otherwise would not be attracted to crochet. Make no mistake, random crocheting is becoming an art form in its own right and should not be confused with pattern making.

The other kind of random crochet is more like sculpture. It can be freestanding or hanging, but artists are now using crochet to create beautiful and stunning pieces of art. Gone are the days when someone crocheted a sampler and hung it in a frame. Crochet sculpture is also really taking hold with artists who also happen to like needle craft and have chosen crochet for its versatility and ability to be crocheted onto wire, rings and almost any structure that will support a sculpture – either hanging or freestanding. So if you aren't into afghans and baby booties, it doesn't necessarily mean that you aren't into crochet.

Crocheters: Busy as Ever!

There are many reasons to crochet, and so crochet is becoming more popular than ever. You would think that in an age of computerized sewing and knitting machines that the average crafter would go in favor of those instead of 'old fashioned' hand crochet but you'd be wrong. People from all walks of life find crochet an incredibly expressive needlecraft, as well as a very personal one. Here are some reasons why so many people crochet:

- Gift giving is a great reason to crochet. Anyone with a credit card can buy a gift, which will be forgotten as soon as it is opened, but a handmade afghan will be kept forever.

- Connect with a daughter, cousin, sister, friend, parent or anyone though learning or teaching crochet.

- Crochet is extremely relaxing and passes the time quickly if you are waiting for a doctor's appointment or someone to arrive at the airport.

- Crochet is inexpensive. You can get started with as little as ten dollars at a department store or a garage sale; or you can get free supplies from a relative or a friend.

- Once you get proficient at crochet. you can watch TV, go on vacation, do laundry, or have a conversation and crochet at the same time!

- You can take crochet with you wherever you go. On long car trips, it is a great way to pass the time.

- Crochet helps keep your fingers nimble. Ask your doctor if there are any medical benefits for your hands when you crochet.

Watch someone crochet the next time you get a chance. You will see that they are at peace, relaxed and probably creating something that will make the world a happier place!

Some Crochet Innovations

While some may think that crochet is outdated and old-fashioned, it is quite alive, modern and growing as a needlecraft. There are new yarns, new techniques and new patterns that have updated crochet and taken it to the next level of creativity and fashion. Here are just a few of the latest trends that make crochet a contemporary needlecraft worth looking into.

Hairpin Lace

Hairpin lace, which was invented in Victorian times, has made a comeback. While it was originally crocheted on hairpins, it is now created on a hairpin loom; and along with new patterns and new yarns it is simply gorgeous. When crocheted together, the fine lace strips that come off the loom can be crocheted together in infinite possibilities to create delicate and feminine tops, sweaters, dresses, shawls, purses and home accessories. The best part of hairpin lace is that all that is needed to create beautiful lace creations is an understanding of the basic crochet stitches.

Tunisian Crochet

Part crochet, part knitting, Tunisian crochet is a form of crochet that produces a distinctive fabric that looks woven. The crochet hook that produces Tunisian is longer than a regular hook and has a stopper on the end. The hook is longer with a stopper because as in knitting, the stitches are left on the hook as they are worked on the first pass and then worked off on the second. Tunisian crochet is also referred to as Afghan crochet. The Tunisian crochet has a Mediterranean feel, especially with the new vibrant colors of yarn available. As well, there are new books with patterns for clothing and home accessories.

Broomstick Crochet

Broomstick crochet produces a beautiful scalloped lace that can be made into scarves, bags, afghans, and other beautiful craft projects. Broomstick crochet can also be used for edgings on other projects.

Broomstick edging is created by looping the thread around and oversized knitting needle and then using a crochet hook to create the lace scallops. It is easy to do for beginners because all you have to know is single crochet.

Crochet with Beads

Crocheting with beads isn't a new idea, but with the new variety and availability of beads and the new colors and types of yarn, it has become a fashionable way to create many chic and modern looking tops and handbags.

Beads of any kind can be used in a pattern effectively to create a beautiful fabric. Many patterns now incorporate beads, or you can simply add beads to your work by threading them onto your yarn before you begin crocheting. Beads can be used to liven up a plain stitch or small beads can be scattered over a lace pattern to create a beautiful motif. The combination of modern beads, patterns, stitches, and yarns creates endless and exquisite possibilities.

Spool crochet

A great project for kids, spool crochet is an old favorite that is making a comeback. The ropelike cord that is produced from spool crochet is also good for using up scrap yarn you may have lying around. As a joint project, kids can crochet the cord and then mom can sew the cord into a coil that can make placemats, potholders, coasters, and dollhouse rugs.

To make the crochet spool, you will need a spool that is made of wood. Nail four brads in a square on the top and you are ready to crochet. To begin, make a slip knot in the yarn and tie it to one of the brads, pushing the end of the yarn down into the hole of the spool.

Next, loop the yarn around each one of the brads. Begin crocheting by passing the yarn around to the first brad with a yarn loop. Use a crochet hook to pull the loop up over the brad and the piece of yarn. The old loop will go down towards the hole in the spool while the long end of the yarn becomes the new loop on the brad. Continue on until you will begin to see a cord appearing out of the bottom of the spool.

You can make the cord as long as you like and even change colors. When the cord has reached the desired length, simply take it off the brad and finish off the cord.

Random Crochet

One of the most creative ways to crochet doesn't require much knowledge of crochet at all. If you know the basic stitches you can take a pattern and make it your own. Random crochet is the art of following the basics of a pattern but changing the gauge, the stitches, or the shaping to make your own customized project.

For example, you can take a hat pattern and start out with the basic size that you want to make, but as you go along you can make it taller, wider, or throw in all different kinds of stitches, beads, or different kinds of yarns. Your one-of-a-kind creation is much more personal than the standard pattern and much more satisfying to make and wear.

Spread the Word; Share Your Love

Crochet is a gift that is easy to share with others. Of course you can always give presents, but there is so much more to sharing crochet than that.

- Share crochet with a family member, especially children who are old enough to appreciate it. Don't worry if you think that they won't be interested because it is old-fashioned. A quick trip around the internet will show you that very hip people are crocheting everything from eerie spider web granny squares to post modern sculpture.

- Donate crochet to fundraisers. Baby sets in particular are extremely popular because everyone wants hand-made heirloom clothes for their children.

●Donate crochet to hospitals. Many new parents can't afford baby clothes. As well, old people who may not have relatives get cold from the air conditioning in hospitals and need things to keep warm. You don't have to make a whole afghan. Usually a throw or a shawl is enough.

●If you have crochet skills start a club or a free workshop. You can even volunteer to go to a community center or a shelter and teach young girls or other women to crochet. Remember, it's a craft where the materials are inexpensive and the girls can take their supplies wherever they go.

Resources A-Bounty!

There are many books on crochet, but if you have access to the internet, it is much easier to go online where you can find video demonstrations, up-to-date information, supplies, patterns, and people who will answer your crochet questions through email. Here are some of the top sites you can go to when you need information or inspiration.

1. http://www.anniescatalog.com/
Anniescatalog.com has new patterns often, so it is a fun site to visit. As well there are crafts, books, beading and jewelry, supplies and magazines.

2. http://www.antiquecrochetpatterns.com/
Antiquecrochetpatterns.com features patterns from a bygone era like old-fashioned baby bonnets as well as capes and hats.

3. http://www.caron.com/
Caron.com is still a manufacturer's site, but it has patterns that are a great cross between the practical and the creative. If you are looking for that pattern that says something special, chances are you will find it here.

4. http://www.coatsandclark.com/
Coatesandclark.com is a manufacturer's website and features all of their patterns, so if you are looking for one of them, you will find it here. This site also offers patterns and information in Spanish

5. http://www.craftbits.com/
Craftbits.com is a community website with lots of patterns and lots of support. It is easy to navigate and you can personalize it with your 'favorites' page.

6. http://crochet.about.com/
About.com has answers for everything and that includes answers for commonly asked questions about crochet. On their various pages, they provide links to hundreds of patterns as well as plenty of their own, along with advice on how to make projects better.

7. http://www.crochetcabana.com/
Crochetcabana.com is a great website for beginners. Here you will find patterns for basic deigns that are easy to make and easy to download.

8. http://www.crochetdesigns.com/
Crochetdesigns.com features mainly patterns for making placemats, coasters, doilies, and table cloths. There are many specialty patterns and software to download that lets you create your own designs.

9. http://www.crochetkitten.com/
Crochetkitten.com brings crochet into the 21st century. The patterns here are limited but there are patterns for cool club clothes and accessories, cat clothes, and cat dolls.

10. http://www.crochetme.com
Crochetme.com is one of the more popular of the crochet community website featuring blogs, forums, patterns, free resources, events and news, magazines and shopping.

11. http://www.crochetpatterncentral.com/
Crochet pattern central has hundred of patterns, alphabetized by project so they are easy to find. As well, most projects have finished pictures so you have an idea of what the finished product will look like.

12. http://crochetworks.tripod.com/
If you are looking for unusual patterns, crochetworks.com has them. This includes holiday projects, gifts for babies, stuffed animals, and interesting home accessories.

13. http://www.dmc-usa.com/
Manufacturing yarns for over 250 years, dmc-usa.com present patterns that challenge different skill levels to make well-thought out and fun projects.

14. http://www.freepatterns.com/
As the name implies, free patterns.com has access to over 2700 crochet patterns. These patterns range from garments to holiday and include home accessories.

15. http://www.freevintagecrochet.com/
As the name implies, the patterns here are from a different era. This website has nostalgic patterns and a free newsletter.

16. http://www.jpfun.com/
The JPF crochet club has patterns as well as activities. There are surveys and online games that earn you points to purchase patterns if they are not already free of charge.

17. http://www.lionbrand.com/
Lionbrand.com is the manufacturer's website, but still provides many popular free patterns as well as podcasts and listings for events, charities and clubs.

18. http://www.nyyarns.com/
In keeping with the tradition of all that is stylish, nyyarns.com combines their dazzling yarns with chic patterns to help you produce great-looking clothes.

19. http://www.patonsyarns.com
Another manufacturer's website, this Canadian company has free patterns in many different categories as well as instruction for crocheters and knitters alike.

20. http://www.ravelry.com/shop
    This website has it all and is probably the most helpful for a beginning crocheter. There are patterns, yarns, hooks, tips, forums, groups, and people who will give you all kinds of advice and support on crocheting or knitting.

Conclusion

    As you can see, crochet is one of the more incredible needle crafts. Unlike its counterparts, crochet has a rich history, is inexpensive and easy to learn, and is extremely versatile. It can be taken anywhere, is very relaxing, and is wonderful to share with others.

    Hopefully, after reading this publication, you will have a different view of crochet and the things that you can accomplish with it. At first, crochet will be tedious, but once you get the hang of it, you will enjoy it for the rest of your life.

    This book covers many of the basics but remember, there is a whole world of crocheters, both local and on the Internet out there. After you master the basics outlined in this publication, feel free to tap into their wisdom so that you continue to grow and make crochet a part of your life that really means something special to you.

CPSIA information can be obtained
at www.ICGtesting.com
Printed in the USA
LVIC06n1729120514
385444LV00002B/20